1 MONTH OF FREE READING

at

www.ForgottenBooks.com

By purchasing this book you are eligible for one month membership to ForgottenBooks.com, giving you unlimited access to our entire collection of over 1,000,000 titles via our web site and mobile apps.

To claim your free month visit: www.forgottenbooks.com/free894398

* Offer is valid for 45 days from date of purchase. Terms and conditions apply.

ISBN 978-0-265-82092-6
PIBN 10894398

This book is a reproduction of an important historical work. Forgotten Books uses state-of-the-art technology to digitally reconstruct the work, preserving the original format whilst repairing imperfections present in the aged copy. In rare cases, an imperfection in the original, such as a blemish or missing page, may be replicated in our edition. We do, however, repair the vast majority of imperfections successfully; any imperfections that remain are intentionally left to preserve the state of such historical works.

Forgotten Books is a registered trademark of FB &c Ltd.
Copyright © 2018 FB &c Ltd.
FB &c Ltd, Dalton House, 60 Windsor Avenue, London, SW19 2RR.
Company number 08720141. Registered in England and Wales.

For support please visit www.forgottenbooks.com

Historic, Archive Document

Do not assume content reflects current scientific knowledge, policies, or practices.

The Evans Specialty Nursery
Arlington, Texas

Special Nut and Fruit Trees

One of our new pecans, four years old, and bore four pounds of nuts

Clark, Cline & Evans

C. H. CLARK　　　W. D. CLINE　　　J. A. EVANS
Wichita Falls　　Wichita Falls　　Arlington

1922—23

The Evans Specialty Nursery
Arlington, Texas

Special Nut and Fruit Trees

One of our new pecans, four years old, and bore four pounds of nuts

Clark, Cline & Evans

C. H. CLARK
Wichita Falls

W. D. CLINE
Wichita Falls

J. A. EVANS
Arlington

1922—23

TO ALL WHO ARE INTERESTED IN BETTER NUTS AND FRUITS, we extend greetings, and request their careful consideration of the following pages of this, our announcement and first little catalog.

We wish to emphasize the word "Specialty" in our name.

The best results can not be secured without specialization, and we have limited our efforts to a few kinds of trees so as to be able to furnish the public the very best of each of these kinds that breeding and selection can produce.

By far the greater portion of our nut and fruit trees are of those kinds we have originated or have collected through many years of search.

No other nursery has these special varieties, and we grow a relatively small proportion of what other nurseries have.

We are not, however, above using other choice varieties than our own, particularly where they may be needed to extend the range of ripening across the entire season.

In addition to our breeding work, we have certain plats of land set aside for the purpose of assembling promising fruits from all parts of the world, and testing them out in our climate; and no doubt we shall be able to announce from time to time, special varieties of merit from this source.

In short, ours is a special nursery, conducted for the purpose of breeding, assembling, and testing out nuts and fruits adapted to the Southwest. And it will be our aim to announce no variety previous to its having shown clear indications of merit.

Our prices are as low as could be expected under the circumstances. We have spared neither expense nor pains to produce the best trees possible to be grown. We use a great deal of fertilizer, and are prepared to irrigate our fruit trees in periods of drought, thus making sure their strength and vigor.

Our manager has spent many years and considerable money in acquiring our superior collection.

Establishing of our nursery was also quite different from establishing an ordinary one. It was necessary for us to set out an orchard and grow buds before we could begin, whereas the ordinary nursery has an unlimited bud supply from any number of sources in the very beginning.

All this requires time and money—particularly in the case of pecans—and it could not be expected that our prices would be on a level with stuff grown without irrigation and fertilizer, and from buds cut from any available tree of a given variety.

It is not our purpose to establish a cheap nursery. We shall employ every means to give the public the very best, and shall expect a reasonable price for our products.

There is no economy in buying a cheap tree. It means too much and lasts too long.

PRICE LIST
1922-23

SPECIAL PEACHES

	Each	Doz.	100
to 3 feet	$ .50	$5.00	$40.00
to 4 feet	.75	8.00	55.00
to 6 feet	1.00	10.00	75.00

STANDARD PEACHES

	Each	Doz.	100
to 3 feet	$ .40	$4.25	$32.00
to 4 feet	.60	6.50	50.00
to 6 feet	.80	8.50	65.00

NECTARINES

	Each	Doz.	100
to 3 feet	$ .60	$6.50	$50.00
to 4 feet	.80	8.50	65.00
to 6 feet	1.00	10.00	80.00

SPECIAL PLUMS

	Each	Doz.	100
to 3 feet	$ .75	$8.00	$55.00
to 4 feet	1.00	10.00	75.00
to 6 feet	1.25	12.00	95.00

STANDARD PLUMS

	Each	Doz.	100
to 3 feet	$ .50	$5.00	$40.00
to 4 feet	.75	8.00	55.00
to 6 feet	1.00	10.00	75.00

SPECIAL PRUNES

	Each	Doz.	100
to 3 feet	$ .75	$8.00	
to 4 feet	1.00	10.00	
to 6 feet	1.25	12.00	

SPECIAL APRICOTS

	Each	Doz.	100
to 3 feet	$ .75	$8.00	
to 4 feet	1.00	10.00	
to 6 feet	1.25	12.00	
PECIAL CHERRY	$ .75	$7.50	

PECANS

Each	Doz.	100

For prices of Pecans see Page 17.

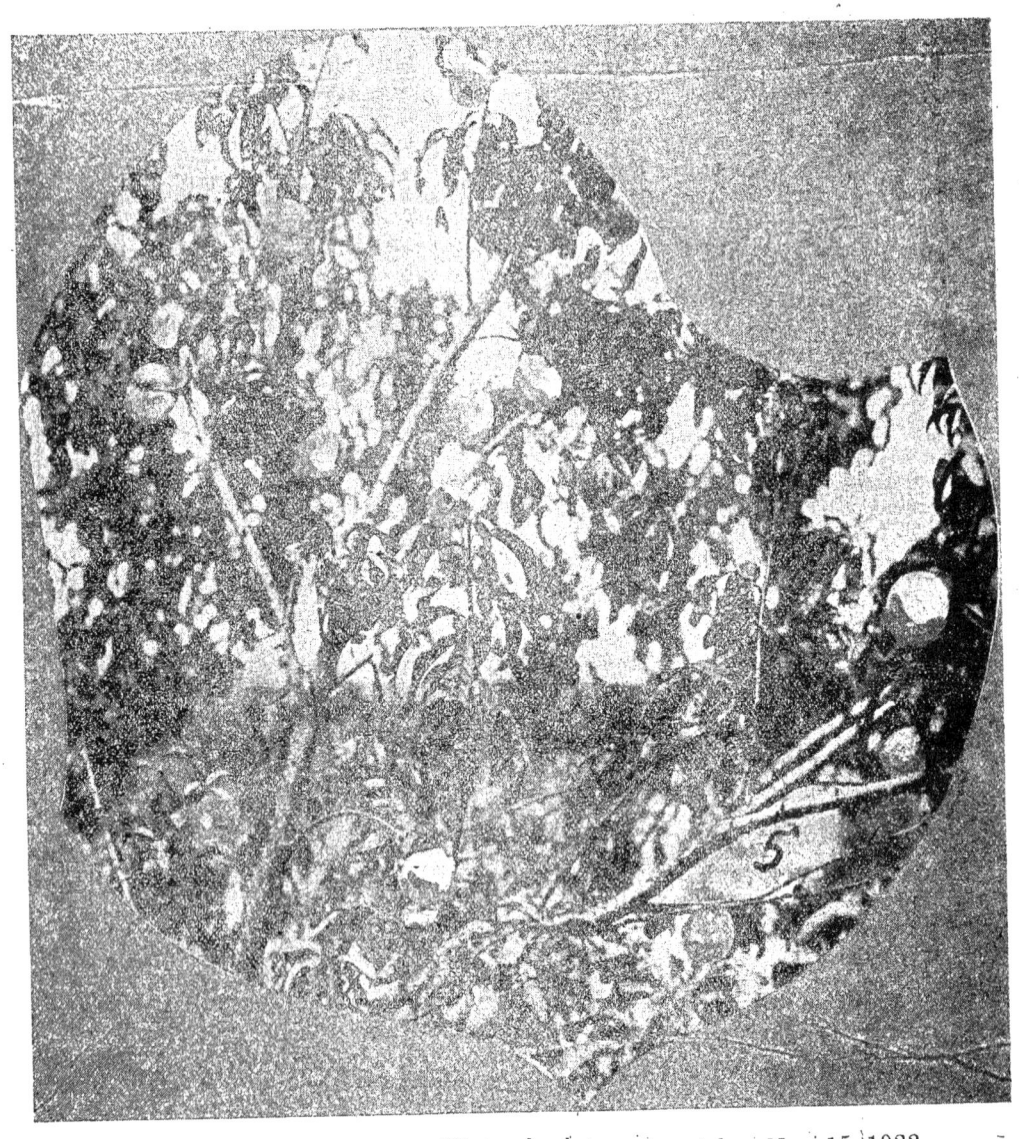

This picture of one of our Wintercheek trees was taken Nov. 15, 1922.

SPECIAL PEACHES

Our manager has for fifteen years been making a collection of superior varieties of peaches; and now, for the first time, we are offering these varieties to the public, together with a few others that have already been introduced.

Each variety has been tested by us, and we do not hesitate to recommend each and every one without reservation.

BRYANT EARLY. F. JUNE 1 TO 10. (Our own introduction). This is the first real peach to ripen that we know of. It is really of most excellent quality for any season, to say nothing of so early a peach. Size, large; color, creamy background with pink to red shading. Flesh creamy white, very juicy and sweet.

We have been searching for a long time for an early peach of real quality, and have found it in the Bryant Early.

BEST JUNE. F. Last of month. Fruit of large size and delicious flavor. Color light with red cheek. A very regular and prolific bearer. Not only its fine qualities but its season of ripening, also, make this a desirable variety.

LANE. C. JULY 10. A large golden yellow fruit, firm, juicy, and sweet. Few others surpass the beauty of a Lane tree when loaded with fruit.

SMITH. F. JULY 15. One of the surest and most prolific bearers ever originated. Fruit sweet and delicious. Every collection should contain Smith.

GOV. LANHAM. C. MID JULY. Yellow, shaded with red. Firm flesh of fine quality. Very large and handsome.

CAMPBELL. C. JULY 20. (Our own introduction.) A peach of large size and magnificent appearance. White, with reddish purple shading extending over much of the surface. Extremely juicy, and deliciously rich and sweet.

ELBERTA. F. LATTER PART OF JULY. (Our own introduction.) This variety is too well known to need any description, but we want to say something about our special Elberta. During several years we made search for the BEST Elberta tree, and think we have found it at last. The tree was old at the time, and we were able to get only a few buds. We have multiplied these buds, however, and our entire stock of Elberta trees has grown from them.

Bud variation is a mooted question, and its discussion is beyond the scope of a brief catalog; but we can not avoid calling attention to the fact that within narrow limits bud variation is infinite. It is probable that, were a thousand different buds put on under exactly similar conditions, the growth from each one would differ somewhat from that of each of the others in size, shape, number of branches, and other particulars. Neither can it be denied that bud variation of wide range occurs occasionally, giving rise to mutations, or "sports."

We are of the opinion that failure to take advantage of bud selection is frequently the cause of the "running out" of varieties.

At any rate, those who argue that one bud of a variety is as good as another are estopped by their own argument from offering trees that will produce superior fruit.

We will not go so far as to say that we have the best Elberta in the world; but we do say that our trees are grown from buds of the most superior tree of the variety we have ever seen or heard of —and it is not a sufficient answer to an inquiring mind to say that this particular tree produced superior fruit because of richer soil or otherwise more favorable location; for it stood in a ten-acre orchard where conditions were as nearly alike as possible, and no other tree in the orchard produced such fruit.

You may be able to buy trees for less money than we will be able to sell you these selected and specially grown ones for, but the best tree is cheapest in the end.

MARGARET EVANS. F. Immediately following Elberta. (Our own introduction.) An Elberta cross that resembles that variety when ripe, but not so while green. Oblong, and more pointed at the apex. Flesh yellow, juicy, and deliciously sweet, by far surpassing the Elberta in quality. Too soft for a good shipping peach, but for home use, to be eaten out of hand, can not be surpassed. Tree does not grow as large as some other kinds, but it is a consistent bearer.

CHARLOTTE EVANS. F. WEEK AFTER ELBERTA. (Our own introduction.) This is probably the most beautiful peach that has ever been originated. A beautiful and peculiar shade of red covers almost the entire surface of the fruit when fully ripe; and one of the trees is a sight to behold with the large red fruit set among the green leaves. Flesh yellow and very firm. Keeps from ten days to two weeks after harvesting. Flavor sub-acid. Quality fine when fully ripe. Fruit colors before ripening, and may lead to premature gathering, but quality and flavor fine when fully ripe.

The very finest canned and preserved fruit we have ever seen were of this kind; and it bids fair to supplant all others for these purposes, as also for shipping.

The tree has not shown itself to be a strong grower in thin sandy soil, but thrives in rich soil, and is a fine black land peach.

Every orchard should contain a liberal proportion of this variety and every yard should have one or two.

When Mr. T. E. Hiett of Arlington saw the original tree loaded with ripe fruit he said: "That is the only real peach tree I have ever seen. All others are things—just things!"

OWETA. F. AUG. 1. (Our own introduction.) Large size, pink cheek on creamy background. Deliciously juicy and sweet.

While the original tree of this variety is still young, and our budded trees have not come into bearing, the excellence of the fruit forces its recommendation in a limited way.

SHORT. F. AUG. 10. (Our own introduction.) **Short** in name only. Of the Elberta type, but larger. Light tinted yellow with red shading. Flesh very tender, juicy, and sweet, much surpassing the Elberta.

This variety originated as a chance seedling, growing from under the edge of a porch of Mr. J. E. Short, from whom we acquired the budding right. Tree a remarkably strong and healthy grower.

Mr. Short makes the following statement: "I selected some peaches from the tree growing by my porch, which Mr. Evans has named the Short, and eleven of these peaches weighed sixteen pounds. These peaches were selected in a favorable season. They are not always that large, but are always extra fine."

ELCLING. C. MID AUGUST. (Of our own introduction.) Of the Elberta type, though a cling. It is not only one of the handsomest peaches grown, but no other surpasses it in quality. Large, nearly round, to slightly oblong. Yellow tinted background with dark red shading. Remarkably juicy, sweet and delicious. Tree a strong and thrifty grower. No orchard or yard complete without this variety.

EVANS. F. AUG. 12. (Our own introduction.) Very large and beautifully shaded. Of the Elberta type, but of superior quality. Fruit from this tree has created a sensation wherever shown. Tree an accidental seedling in the yard of Mrs. B. C. Evans of Fort Worth, for whom the variety is named.

AUGUSTA. F. AUG. 15. Also of the Elberta type, but ripens nearly a month later. Very fine quality, and a sure bearer.

SAVAGE QUEEN. F. SEPT. 20. (Our own introduction.) Of the Elberta type, and as large as the largest of that variety. Flesh yellow, very juicy and fine. This is a classy peach in every particular, and the date of its ripening makes it a valuable sort. Tree is a strong healthy grower in both black and sand land, and begins bearing early.

OCTOBERTA. F. OCT. 1. Also of the Elberta family. Of good size, and very fine quality. Valuable on account of its late ripening.

WINTERCHEEK. C. NOV. 15. (Our own introduction). Probably the latest of all peaches to ripen. White with red veined shading. Flesh firm and white, but red near seed. Flavor fine, and fruit very fragrant. Resembles Stinson's October, but fruit larger and of better quality. On trees growing side by side fruit twice as large this year. Trees of this kind grow larger and thriftier than any other, and are the surest and most prolific bearers of all. Blooms late, and seems to escape frost. Have wrapped the fruit like oranges and kept till Christmas. Have experimented with this variety for ten years, and the fruit has never been injured by frost in the fall. During October, 1918, there were two heavy freezes, and the peaches froze on the trees. Failure to set a crop has not occurred during the ten years, and this was the only crop lost. In fact the trees bear so heavily that severe thinning is absolutely necessary to attain size in the fruit and to protect the tree from the over-production of seed.

We regard this variety as one of the most valuable additions to horticulture.

STANDARD PEACHES

In addition to our special peaches, before described, we grow a few of the Mayflower and Mamie Ross to fill in.

MAYFLOWER. MAY 20. Usually classed as a freestone, but not perfectly so. One of the earliest peaches to ripen, and, when fully ripe, red all over. Flesh white to the seed. Usually described as a fine early peach, but we can not say very much as to its quality. It is much better than no peach, and for that reason every collection should contain a few.

MAMIE ROSS. SEMI-C. JULY 4. Too well known to need much description. A large white and red peach that bears well and is of fine quality.

SPECIAL NECTARINES

It is a source of wonder to us that so little of this delightful and attractive fruit is grown; but in our part of the state, at least, very few people have ever seen one. So we will say, in simple language, that a nectarine is a peach with the skin of a plum, possessing a peculiar rich flavor of its own. We have spared no pains to get the best possible collection, and we urge the public to try them.

HUMBOLDT. AUGUST. Of the very largest size, bright orange color, mottled and shaded with dark crimson on sunny side. Flesh orange-colored, tender, juicy and very rich. Tree a reasonably vigorous grower, and a heavy bearer.

ADVANCE. JULY. Large and round, with green skin on shaded portions. Blotched with reddish-brow where the sun gets in. Flesh green-tinted white, very sweet and rich. Not so rank a tree as the Humboldt, but healthy and a good bearer.

STANWICK. AUG. A very large fruit, with pale skin that is shaded with violet. Flesh is white, tender and juicy. Probably the best shipping and canning nectarine. Tree a strong healthy grower.

ANSENNE. Furnished us by the U. S. Department of Agriculture through the Bureau of Plant Exploration. Sent from New Zealand. Our tree is too young to bear yet, but the following description is given by the Department: "Large, red, free stone fruits of splendid appearance and excellent flavor. Bears freely."
(We have only a few small trees—forced buds of 1922.)

TURKESTAN. Furnished us by the U. S. Department of Agriculture through the Bureau of Plant Exploration. We call it Turkestan because it came from there, and bore no name.
The Department describes it as follows: "Fruits large, freestone, creamy yellow with red blush. The flesh is creamy white, red at stone, juicy, crisp, subacid and of very good quality. Skin rather tough, but parts readily from the flesh. A good shipper."
(We have only a few small trees—forced buds of 1922.)

LIST OF SPECIAL PLUMS

APEX PLUMCOT. F. JUNE. Supposed to be a cross between an apricot and plum. Fruit is very large, crimson in color, and parts readily from the seed. The flesh is yellow, rich, and oramatic. Tree is a strong compact grower, and bears well even where apricots can not be grown. Ripens with earliest plums.

ADVANCE. MAY 15. A Texas seedling of great value. Tree is remarkably healthy and vigorous. Fruit is red, firm, and large. One of the most profitable for market.

McCARTNEY, MAY 15. A large yellow plum of fine quality for the season.

OXHEART. JUNE 1. A thrifty tree that produces large bright red fruit that is sweet and fine.

DORIS. JUNE 10. A large plum that is nearly round, and dark red. Deliciously sweet, with thin but strong skin. Bore in our nursery row this season.

GONZALES. JULY 1 TO 10. A fine brilliant red plum. Firm and juicy, with a pleasant sweet flavor. A good keeper and shipper. Tree strong and healthy in Texas climate, and a sure and early bearer. Do not leave this variety out of your collection.

MONTHALIA, JULY 1. This variety originated as a Texas seedling and is adapted to this climate. It is a sure bearer of large, round, yellow-red fruit.

SULTAN, JULY 1 TO 10. A large purplish red plum of fine quality. Bears young and abundantly.

GIANT. AUG. The name is significant, as it is of enormous size. Yellow background with dark crimson shading. Flesh firm, sweet, delicious.

WADE'S OCTOBER. SEPT.-OCT. This variety resembles our ordinary wild plum in both tree and fruit. It is probably a cross between a wild plum and some other. Bears very heavy crops of fruit that is somewhat larger and better than the wild plum. Valuable for jams and jellies and for its season of ripening.

LIST OF STANDARD PLUMS

EXTRA EARLY CHERRY. MAY. A bright red plum of the Myrobolan type, with brisk and pleasing flavor. Not large, but an abundant bearer. Originated as a seedling in California. Our test tree is extremely thrifty, with total absence of disease. The only trouble we fear with this kind is too early blooming.

BEAUTY. JUNE. Recently introduced, but has already won its place. Crimson colored fruit with amber colored flesh. One of the largest early plums. Tree a reasonably vigorous grower and heavy bearer.
Note: This is not the yellow plum sold under similar name.

BARTLETT. ABOUT JULY 1. Red colored fruit of a good size dotted with yellow spots. We regard its quality as the highest. It has a very peculiar and distinctive flavor, resembling that of a Bartlett pear. The tree also grows in shape like a pear tree, and might easily be mistaken for one when young. A strong and healthy grower with us, and a young and prolific bearer. From seed planted in our nursery in the spring of 1921, and the resulting trees budded in June, of the same year, quite a number bore fruit in 1922.
If we could grow only four plum trees, one would be a Bartlett.

CLYMAN. JULY. Large, with dry, sweet and firm flesh. A reddish tinted purple with blue bloom.

AMERICA. JULY 10. Yellowish red plum of fair to large size, and good quality. An enormous bearer, and generally recognized as one of the good plums for Texas.

BURBANK. JULY 15. Large, firm, and red, slightly mottled. Bears young and is very prolific.

ARKANSAS LOMBARD. JULY 15. Medium size, round, red and good—and sure to bear a crop.

SHIRO. JULY. A large yellow plum, with fine firm flesh, which makes it a good keeper. Our test tree is very vigorous, showing it to be adapted to this section.

NONA. AUG. 1. A large bright red plum, with juicy flesh of fine quality. Bears heavy crops, beginning early. Bore in our nursery row this season.

WICKSON. AUG. A very large heart-shaped plum. Yellow, shaded with carmine and covered with white bloom. Flesh firm, sugary and delicious. Fruit keeps for a long time, and the tree is one of the most vigorous growers.

GRAND DUKE. AUG. A very large dark purple plum, coated with bloom of blue. Quality good, being rich and sweet when ripe.

GAVIOTA. AUG. Fruit round to oblong, with clear yellow flesh that is very fragrant and sweet. Seed extremely small.

KELSEY'S JAP. AUG. Size, large; color, greenish-yellow, disposed to be red on sunny side; firm flesh, juicy, with rich vinous flavor.

SATSUMA. AUG. Fruit nearly round and dark red. Flesh same color as skin, firm, of fair flavor, and pit small. Very productive.

GOLDEN BEAUTY. AUG. Our stock of this kind was budded from a tree we found growing on the place. All who see the fruit say it is much larger than ordinary Golden Beauty. It is one of the surest and heaviest bearers, and its keeping qualities are truly remarkable. It is very fine for jellies and other plum products, and every orchard should contain some of these trees.

COE'S GOLDEN DROP. SEPT. A large, yellow, oval plum with rich, firm, sweet flesh.

YELLOW EGG. SEPT. The name tells the story of color and shape. Inclined to acidity till fully ripe, when it becomes sweet.

BAVØY'S GREEN GAGE. SEPT. Greenish-yellow, round and large. Fine flavor, and highly recommended for canning.

PRESIDENT. SEPT. An English plum. Fruit large, purple and egg-shaped. Flesh yellow, and of fine texture and flavor. A very promising market plum.

OCTOBER PURPLE. OCT. 1. This is a purple plum, as the name implies. Our test tree came from New York, where the variety is highly esteemed. It bore its first crop this season, but on account of the protracted drought, the fruit did not attain expected size, though the same objection could be urged against other late kinds.

We have grown only a limited number of trees and think them worth a trial.

SPECIAL PRUNES

We grow only two varieties of prunes, but they are of the highest sugar content, and are otherwise of the finest quality to be found in the world.

The trees in our test grounds are just as thrifty and healthy as any of our plums, and bore well the second year. This seems to indicate that we do not have to send to California for prunes if we are willing to grow them ourselves—at least in this part of the state.

Order a few trees, and be a pioneer in your section.

SUGAR. AUG. Large fruit, extremely rich and sugary. Very tender skin and yellow flesh. Light purple at first, with green shading, changing later to dark purple, covered with white bloom. Probably the sweetest of all prunes. Reported to contain nearly 24 per cent sugar in California, and will contain more here than there. Our test tree bore the second year, is very thrifty, and shows absolutely no sign of disease. We think this may prove a valuable addition to the horticulture of Texas.

IMPERIAL EPINEUSE. (Clairac Mammoth). AUG. Said to be the largest and finest prune grown in California. Light purplish-red, thin skin, and very sweet. Analysis shows 20.4 per cent sugar, while the average French prune shows 18.53. It is reported that 60 to 80 per cent of the dried prunes of this variety will average from 20 to 30 to the pound. Trees in our test plot are thrifty and free from disease.

Jujube tree in its fourth year. The fruit broke its branches the third year in spite of tying and propping.

JUJUBES

JUJUBES (ZIZYPHUS). Introduced by the U. S. Department of Agriculture through the Bureau of Plant Exploration. Sure to prove a most valuable addition to our horticulture.

A beautiful tree with bright shiny leaves, somewhat like chittim, but thicker foliage. Tree is very hardy, and bears young and abundantly. Fruit is brown when ripe, and varies in shape (according to variety) from apple to pear. Some fruits are two inches long, and an inch or more in diameter. Texture and flavor of choice varieties like a fine apple. Good to eat fresh, to preserve, or to be put up like sugared dates. A few seedlings of this fruit were introduced some twenty years ago. Do not confuse them with the improved kinds.

We have one particular variety that so far surpasses all others that we intend to bud from it almost altogether.

We have no trees for sale this season, but expect to be ready next fall.

SPECIAL APRICOTS

Apricots seem to be an exception to the general rule that it pays to fertilize and cultivate fruit trees. They seem to do best in out-of-the-way corners, where the soil is not too rich and the clay is near the surface, and where the ground is sloping.

The trees grow luxuriantly under cultivation in deep rich soil, but they refuse to bear under these conditions.

The apricot is such a delicious fruit that it would be universally grown if it could be made to fruit easily.

We have gathered our collection from many parts of the world, giving particular attention to habits of fruiting; and we are confident that all who buy them will be more than pleased, provided a little thought be given to the place of setting the trees.

TILTON. JULY. Large oval fruit sometimes slightly compressed. Firm yellow flesh that parts readily from the seed. Thrifty grower and heavy bearer. Escapes injury by frost more often than most other kinds.

BARRY. JULY. Said to be one of the best apricots grown. Good size; orange yellow with pink shading; smooth skin and small seed; very prolific.

APRICOT PLUM. Furnished us by the U. S. Department of Agriculture through the Bureau of Plant Exploration, with the following description: "This species produces a very delicious, golden yellow fruit with reddish blush. The fruit is about 2 inches in diameter. Seems to be a good shipper." It comes from Shantung, China.

(We have only a few small trees—forced buds of 1922.)

JAPANESE APRICOT. Furnished us by the U. S. Department of Agriculture through the Bureau of Plan Exploration, with the following description: "A tree resembling the common apricot, and probably hybridizing with it. Blooms very early, producing white to deep crimson, fragrant flowers. Fruits used extensively in Japan, producing one of the sourest pickles known, and forming part of the Japanese soldiers' ration. There are many selected flowering varieties of superb beauty in China and Japan."

(We have only a few forced buds of 1922.)

CHERRIES

Cherries, as a rule, have not been a great success in Texas, but we found a Texas seedling that has not missed a crop in fifteen years. It is of the eastern or sour cherry class, as opposed to the California cherry, though it is almost sweet.

The fruit when fully ripe is nearly black, and resembles the black heart cherries of the Carolinas and Virginia.

The tree is a remarkably vigorous grower. The ones in our test grounds are now three years old, and are much larger than any other tree of any kind that is the same age. Some of them commenced bearing the second year, and all bore the third.

It is yet too soon for us to place our moral warrant back of the performance of the variety, but the great vigor and beauty of the tree induces us to offer a few to the public.

We have only about a hundred sprouts from the roots of the old trees—and they will, of course, come true.

PECANS

The following cuts show some of our special varieties of pecans.

36 to the pound—51.7 per cent meat.

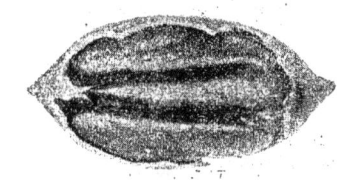

65 per cent meat—very rich. Highest of all grades.

58 per cent meat. Extremely rich. Not subject to scab.

56 per cent meat. Very handsome.

60 per cent meat, and tree most beautiful.

The most special thing about our special nursery is pecans. Our general manager has made a close study of the different phases of pecan culture for many years, and he has made a most extensive investigation of native Texas varieties. In addition to his previous studies, he was for some years pecan specialist to the Extension Department of the Texas A. & M. College, and his travels in that capacity afforded unequaled opportunity for further study and observation.

Up to the present time practically all the introduced varieties of so-called "paper shell" pecans (we do not use the word) have originated as chance seedlings, no systematic or sustained effort at breeding having been carried out.

There are by far many more wild pecan trees in Texas than in all other states and countries combined, and it is a source of wonder that thorough search of these trees had not been made sooner in order to get superior Texas pecans for Texas. Of course something had been done along this line, and some highly meritorious varieties introduced—and posterity will recognize its debt of gratitude to H. A. Halbert, E. E. Risien, J. H. Burkett and others—but our manager has conducted the most thorough and extended search, probably, and has collected, and is now engaged in growing, varieties of such surpassing excellence that we are confident they will place Texas on a new basis in pecan culture.

Pecans are divided into two classes, which we naturally term the eastern and the western. These classes differ each from the other in growth habit of tree, and in other respects. Discussion of these differences would be too long for a catalog. As a general rule the eastern kinds should be planted in East Texas and the western kinds in Central and West Texas.

Most of our stock is of the western varieties, though we carry the eastern also.

We show above pictures of some of our new varieties, though all our trees of these kinds were contracted months ago. However, we retained a thousand trees to get buds from; and we expect to be able to furnish them in great numbers in the future.

At present we offer the following varieties for sale:

HALBERT (Western). Good size, shin shell, cracks easily, has good flavor, and is 57½ per cent meat. This is the earliest and most prolific bearer of all varieties yet brought to public notice. Its one fault is its great susceptibility to fungous diseases. For this reason it should not be planted east of Dallas. Even in that locality it scabs in flat bottom lands during rainy seasons. It should be included in every planting west of Dallas.

BURKETT (Western). A very large round nut of thin shell and easy cracking and separating. Has a good flavor, and is 56½ per cent meat. Does not bear so young and so heavily as the Halbert, but the tree is a rank grower and a consistent bearer. Much more resistant to fungous diseases than the Halbert. Trees doing well as far east as Shereveport.

TEXAS PROLIFIC (Western). A large oblong nut of moderately thin shell and fair cracking quality. It is one of the richest of all pecans, as it is more than 50 per cent meat. The tree is one of the youngest and most prolific bearers and is fairly resistant to fungous diseases.

STUART (Eastern). The oldest of the introduced varieties, and therefore the best known. A large oblong nut, somewhat flattened at the apex, with dark stripes running to the point. Medium shell, and only fair cracking and separating qualities. Tree a vigorous, upright grower, and perfectly healthy over entire pecan territory. 47 per cent meat.

DELMAS (Eastern). A large smooth oblong nut, gently sloping at both ends. Medium shell, and of good cracking and separating qualities. Tree a vigorous grower, but subject to scab in damp climates. However, this trouble need not be feared in Central and West Texas, as those sections are practically immune from fungous disases, except in rare instances with varieties brought from the west. The Delmas is possibly the best of the eastern kinds for black upland. 50.4 per cent meat.

SUCCESS (Eastern). A very large blunt nut, much enlarged at the base and slightly flattened at the apex. Medium shell, and of good cracking and separating qualities. Trees not so vigorous as the Delmas, but a consistent bearer, and considered 'one of the best in Georgia and the Gulf states. 53 per cent meat.

SCHLEY (Eastern). The real "class" of the eastern varieties. In fact it is in a class by itself over there, bringing a higher price than any other eastern kind. It is the only eastern pecan that belongs in the class of our best new western ones.

A long nut of good size, slightly shouldered, and tapering to a point at both ends. Shell very thin, and cracking and separating qualities very high. The tree is vigorous enough, but a rather shy bearer. The nuts sometimes pop open and sprout on the trees during rainy falls in the coastal regions, though this need not be feared in Central and West Texas. 61.4 per cent meat.

PRICES

From $1.00 each, up to $3.00, with 10 per cent reduction by the hundred, and 20 per cent by the thousand.

The value of a pecan tree can not be accurately measured by the growth from the bud. A late bud on a large thrifty stock may be only 1 foot long, while an early bud on a smaller stock may be 3 feet long.

The former tree might be more valuable. This is not true to so great an extent with fruit trees, as they all require budding when young, and the length of growth from the bud is nearer to an accurate measure.

The majority of our pecan trees are about the $1.50 size.

We selected our land with the view to its adaptability to a pecan nursery. Our surface soil is of loose sand some twenty-four to thirty inches deep, and is underlaid by a clay subsoil that stops the tap root. Nearly all our trees are dug with the tap roots whole.

Much has been said about the benefit of cutting the tap root of a pecan tree before transplanting. It is urged that from three to five tap roots will put out in place of the one cut—and from three to five are better than one. Might as well say that from three to five dimes are better than a half dollar. It is strange that nature did not have sense enough to make from three to five tap roots in the beginning.

It is also argued that cutting the tap root stimulates the growth of the lateral roots. Doubtless this is true provided the tree lives after transplanting; but one who argues that a pecan tree stands as good a chance to live after a severe operation on the tap root as another tree does with the tap root whole, either knows or cares very little about what he says—and maybe both.

We feel safe in saying that more than half of all the pecan trees set out in Texas have died. We obviate the necessity of severely cutting the tap roots of our trees by the nature of the subsoil. At the same time, stimulation of the lateral root system, in the loose soil above, is effected by checking the tap root below—in other words, WE effect the development of the lateral root system, before you buy the tree, by checking the tap root, and not by cutting it; while, on the other hand, some others would urge YOU to develop a lateral root system, after you buy the tree, by cutting the tap root. This latter method makes the tree easier to dig, easier to set out—and easier to die.

No one can offer you a better root system than we grow.

WHERE TO SET OUT PECAN TREES

In just what kind of soil, and under what conditions, it will pay to set out a pecan tree is worth consideration.

Some one has said that a pecan tree will grow, within its climatic range, anywhere that any other tree will grow.

This statement is largely true if you place plenty of emphasis on the word TREE. It is not at all true that a pecan tree will grow and PRODUCE FRUIT in all such places. The tree must first live and grow—and must grow to live—and after that the margin can be devoted to fruit production.

It requires much mineral plant food material to produce such rich concentrated food as the pecan kernel; and to get these materials requires rich land of loose texture. The rich soil contains the food materials, and the loose texture permits the development of a root system that can reach out and get them.

We grew a fine pecan tree on top of a clay hill by digging a well 5 feet in diameter and 10 feet deep, and filling it with rich soil. Such a tree could not otherwise have grown there. Between this extreme, on the one hand, and a deep, loose alluvial fill with clay subsoil on the other, lies all shades of conditions.

Generally speaking, a few pecan trees can be successfully grown around almost any home with a little trouble and expense. A commercial pecan orchard is, however, a different proposition. That should not be undertaken except in the most favorable soil to be found—and this determined by some one competent to judge.

We do not want to sell pecan trees and have them prove a fallur, as that would retard the development of the industry.

Success is as sure to follow good pecan soil and adapted varieties as failure is to follow the absence of these two necessary conditions.

HOW TO SET OUT A PECAN TREE

Holes for setting pecan trees should be 4½ feet long, 2 feet wide, and 2½ feet deep. If the tip of the tap root requires a greater depth than 2½ feet, it can be secured by the use of the post hole digger in the center of the bottom of the main hole. It is better to provide for the tap root in this manner than it is to cut off part of it.

Of course, the main hole could be dug 3 feet deep or more; but the bottom part of the hole is the expensive part.

An oblong hole is recommended because it permits free use of the shovel handle. It is very difficult to dig a three-foot square hole below 18 inches.

When the trees arrive do not set them in a corner of the garage for a month, but set them out immediately. Take them to the field in the original package. Take out one tree at a time, keeping the roots of the others covered with wet sacks. Before setting tree, trim all bruised and broken parts of roots with a sharp knife, cutting upward with a slant.

Let one man get in the hole with the tree while another shovels in the dirt, using only the good surface soil next to the roots. The man in the hole should keep the roots opened out horizontally, and should pack the dirt in carefully around them with his hands. This will make a cone shaped pile of dirt around the tree in the hole. If fertilizer is used, let it be well rotted stable manure, placed in the ends and at the sides of the hole around this cone, and not in contact with the roots.

When the hole is nearly full, pour in two buckets of water, and allow to settle. Finish filling, and pack down.

Now comes the hard part. Cut off most of the beautiful top of the tree, leaving three or four good plump buds on the budded portion, and pile dirt around the stub to the height of a foot or more. Stick a short piece of board in the ground six inches from the tree on the west side, and another on the south. Keep the ground around the tree stirred once each week. The boards will break the force of the afternoon sun, preventing sun-scald, and the broken ground will conserve moisture.

If you follow these directions carefully, your trees will live.

We are anxious to be of assistance in promoting the development of the pecan industry, and we invite you to write us about your problems.

We will not annoy you by urging you to buy trees from us.

Bearing in nursery now. One of these trees, budded in 1921, bore 58 nuts in 1922. Another, only nine inches high, bore one cluster.